Vintage Alps

ADRIATISCHES MEER
LIGURISCHES MEER
Golf v. Genua
Golf v. Venedig
Venedig
Chioggia
Triest
Istrien
Pola
Rimini
Ravenna
Bologna
Ferrara
Florenz
Livorno
Pistoja
Siena
Genua
Savona
Spezia
Turin
Asti
Vercelli
Mailand
Monza
Bergamo
Brescia
Verona
Vicenza
Treviso
Padua
Cremona
Mantua
Piacenza
Parma
Modena
Reggio
Zürich
Basel
Bern
München
Udine
Görz
Laibach
Fiume
Eisenbahnen, Kanäle
Alpenstraßen, Pässe, Kurorte
Wallfahrtsorte, Festungen
Schlösser, Ruinen
Höhen und Tiefen in Metern
Maßstab 1:4500000
km
2. Maßst. 1:500000
Gr.Glockner
3. Maßst. 1:500000
Göschenen
Andermatt
Galenstock
St. Gotthard

Daniela Horvath | Michael Martinek

VINTAGE ALPEN

Die Bilder unserer Kindheit | When we were young

METROVERLAG

INTRO

Which of us does not enjoy the memory of carefree childhood days in the country, rays of sunshine on their milk-white city-dweller's face and the delicate scent of fresh hay in an Alpine pasture? It is reasonable to suspect that after being taken completely by surprise by the success of "Vintage Vienna" we had worked out a carefully considered concept for "Vintage Alps", but this does not match with the truth.

Instead this book is once again the accidental result of our search and yearning for the perfect picture of an Alpine pasture for one's own living room in an urban setting. Motivated by our publishers and fond collector friends like Wolfgang Weihs, Rudolf Ehrenreich and Hans Einar Johannessen we decided to compile the most charming private Alpine and mountain photographs in cooperation with you, our many contributors and loyal companions on our exciting journey through time.

It was really more important to us to highlight the special charm of the pictures, their imperfect aspect, instead of technique and sheer photographic quality. Therefore over the course of the following pages you may come across unfocussed or even blurred shots now and again. However, from our point of view these personal shots open a fascinating gateway to another time, and give us insight into our parents' and grandparents' world, which was probably not always as idyllic as most snaps show it to be. A time that we now perceive as stylish and exciting again, not least because of pastel shades and TV series like "Mad Men". Incidentally, we also allowed ourselves to add a handfull of rarer black and white photographic documents of earlier Alpine adventures to bring our publishers to despair regarding the conceptualisation for this book.

We look forward to all the further treasures which may still be slumbering in family albums and hope that our time machine in book form reawakens many lovely memories.

Wishing you lots of fun with the pages to follow,

Daniela Horvath & Michael Martinek

VORWORT

Wer erinnert sich nicht gerne an unbeschwerte Kindertage auf dem Land, Sonnenstrahlen im milchigen Großstadtgesicht und den zarten Duft von frischem Heu auf einer Alm? Es könnte nun der Verdacht naheliegen, dass wir für „Vintage Alpen", nach dem für uns völlig überraschenden Erfolg von „Vintage Vienna", ein wohl überlegtes Konzept ausgearbeitet haben, aber es entspricht nicht der Wahrheit. Vielmehr ist dieses Buch wieder das zufällig entstandene Ergebnis unserer Suche und Sehnsucht nach dem perfekten Almidylle-Bild für den eigenen, städtischen Wohnraum.

Motiviert durch unseren Verlag und liebgewonnene Sammler-Freunde wie Wolfgang Weihs, Rudolf Ehrenreich und Hans Einar Johannessen haben wir uns entschlossen, gemeinsam mit euch, den zahlreichen Einsendern und treuen BegleiterInnen auf unserer aufregenden Zeitreise, die charmantesten Privatfotografien aus der Berg- und Alpenwelt zusammenzustellen.

Uns ging es einmal mehr darum den besonderen Charme der Bilder, das Unperfekte, in den Vordergrund zu rücken, weniger die Technik und die reine Fotoqualität. So kann es mitunter vorkommen, dass Sie im Laufe der folgenden Buchseiten auf unscharfe, gar verwackelte Aufnahmen stoßen. Aus unserer Sicht öffnen diese Privataufnahmen jedoch ein faszinierendes Tor zu einer anderen Zeit und geben Einblick in die Welt unserer Eltern und Großeltern, die wohl nicht immer so idyllisch war, wie es uns die meisten Schnappschüsse vermitteln. Eine Zeit, die wir heute nicht zuletzt aufgrund von Pastelltönen und TV-Serien wie „Mad Men" wieder als „stylish" und aufregend empfinden. Wir haben uns übrigens erlaubt, auch eine Handvoll rarer, schwarz-weißer Fotodokumente von frühen alpinen Abenteuern beizumengen, um unseren Verlag ob der Konzeptfindung für dieses Buch völlig zur Verzweiflung zu bringen.

Wir freuen uns auf alle weiteren Schätze, die noch in Familienalben schlummern mögen und hoffen mit unserer Zeitmaschine in Buchform neuerlich viele schöne Erinnerungen wachzurufen.

Viel Freude mit den folgenden Seiten,

Daniela Horvath & Michael Martinek

AUF IN DIE SOMMER-FRISCHE

OFF TO A SUMMER GETAWAY

8

Wer vor dem heißen Sommer in der Stadt fliehen wollte, den zog es in die Sommerfrische in die kühleren Berge. Der Begriff stammt vermutlich aus dem Italienischen „prendere il fresco“ und ist erstmals aus der Bozener Gegend überliefert. Von dort aus verbreitete sich ab Mitte des 19. Jahrhunderts die Praxis der Sommerfrische über den ganzen deutschsprachigen Raum. Wie schön war und ist es doch, den Sommer im Salzkammergut, am Semmering oder auf der Rax , auf dem Ritten oder in Kastelruth am Schlern zu verbringen. Und der Weg dorthin bedeutet für so manchen Städter ein richtiges Abenteuer!

If you wanted to escape from the hot urban summer you were drawn to a summer getaway in the cooler mountains. The term supposedly originates from the Italian "prendere il fresco", and is first recorded in the Bolzano area. From the mid-nineteenth century the practice of the summer getaway spread across the entire German-speaking region. How lovely it was, and still is, to spend summer in the Salzkammergut, in Semmering or at the Rax, on the Ritten or in Kastelruth am Schlern. And the journey to get there holds a real adventure in store for many a town-dweller!

Nach Österreich

Es waren die Ausflugsfahrten am Wochenende, die das Leben versüßten – umso mehr, wenn man die österreichischen Berge einer Düsseldorfer Freundin aus Kriegstagen zeigen konnte, die noch dazu als Souvenir einen Strauß selbst gepflückter Blumen mitnehmen durfte. Hinterstoder 1976.

It was the weekend excursions that made life sweeter – all the more so if you could show the Austrian mountains to a wartime friend from Düsseldorf, who could also pick herself a bunch of flowers to take away as a souvenir. Hinterstoder 1976.

12

Ein Sommerurlaubsausflug um 1965. Über den Jaufenpass geht es von Sterzing ins verschlafene St. Leonhard im Passeiertal. Hier oben bläst der Wind und gelegentlich kämpfte man mit einem flauen Gefühl im Magen nach 39 Kilometern Kurvenfahrt.

A summer holiday trip around 1965. The route leads via the Jaufenpass from Sterzing to sleepy St. Leonhard in the Passeier Valley. It is windy up here, and you occasionally had to fight a queasy feeling in your stomach after 39 kilometres of driving around bends.

Ebenfalls in den 1960ern blickten hier zwei norwegische Buben mit ihrer Mutter in der Gegend bei Hermagor vom Guggenberg ins Tal. Im Hintergrund links erkennt man den Roßkofel (2240m), rechts den Trogkofel (2280m) und den Zweikofel (2059m).

Also in the 1960s: here two Norwegian lads in the Hermagor area with their mother had a view from Guggenberg into the valley. In the background to the left the Roßkofel (2240 m) can be seen, and to the right the Trogkofel (2280 m) and Zweikofel (2059 m).

14

Eine schwarz-weiße Zeitreise in den Sommer 1958 nach Hermagor im Kärntner Gailtal. Idyllisch. Zu sehen: die über 300 Jahre alte St. Ulrichskapelle am Guggenberg.

A black and white journey through time to summer 1958 and Hermagor in the Gail Valley, Carinthia. Idyllic. The over 300 year-old St. Ulrich's Chapel at Guggenberg is visible.

Eine kurze Rast, bevor es wieder „freie Fahrt“ heißt, und es mit der Erkundigungstour durch das Gailtal weitergeht.

A short rest before the "green light" to continue with this trip exploring the Gail Valley.

Linke Seite: Sommerurlaub in Kärnten gegen Ende der 1950er-Jahre in der Gegend um die Koschuta. Ein weiterer stimmungsvoller Schnappschuss aus einem norwegischen Familienalbum. Hinweis für Autofreunde: rechts ein Borgward Isabella und links ein Ford Taunus.

Unten: Als Belohnung für den anstrengenden Ausflug gibt's Kakao und Kuchen und ein Erinnerungsfoto.

Left page: summer holiday in Carinthia around the end of the nineteen-fifties in the area around the Koschuta. Another atmospheric snap from a Norwegian family album. A tip for car lovers: on the right a Borgward Isabella, and on the left a Ford Taunus.

Below: hot chocolate and cake and a keepsake photograph as a reward for the demanding trip.

Dank Selbstauslöser eines der wenigen Fotos der gesamten Familie mitsamt Papa, der sonst für gewöhnlich hinter der Kamera steht. Hier um 1960 auf einem Almgasthof am Großglockner.

Here, thanks to timed shutter release, is one of the few photographs of the entire family together with Dad, who is otherwise usually behind the camera. This is at an inn by an Alpine Pasture at the Großglockner around 1960.

Links: Was für ein Anblick. Die drei Zinnen (Tre Cime di Lavaredo) in Südtirol in den 1960ern.

Unten: Im Winter 1963 mit dem Auto unterwegs nach Hochfügen im Zillertal.

Rechts: Ein Ausflug nach Eisenerz, 1955.

Left: what a view. The Tre Cime di Lavaredo in South Tyrol in the nineteen-sixties.

Below: on the way to Hochfügen in the Zillertal by car in the winter of 1963.

Right page: A Trip to Eisenerz, 1955.

Erzbergbau - Eisenerz
Mittel ERP-Hilfe

Die Jause im Stehen eingenommen (sie ein Keli, er ein Bier), als Tisch der Kofferraumdeckel eines wunderschönen Peugeots – so zeigen sich die Alpen der Pyhrn-Priel-Region von ihrer besten Seite.

Snack break standing up (a Keli for her, a beer for him), and the boot lid of a beautiful Peugeot as a table – the Alps of the Pyhrn-Priel region are showing us their best side here.

Der Großglockner aus interessanter Perspektive. Der Tunnelblick bekommt hier eine neue Bedeutung.

Rechte Seite: Die Großglocknerstraße Anfang der 1960er-Jahre. Weit und breit keine Autos zu sehen.

The Großglockner from an interesting perspective. Here the tunnel view takes on a new meaning.

Right page: the Großglockner road at the beginning of the nineteen-sixties. No cars to be seen for miles.

Unten: Eine Bergwanderung um 1971 auf der Tiroler Nordkette. Man sieht, dass es auch mit dezentem Schuhwerk möglich war.

Below: a mountain walk around 1971 up the north mountain chain in Tyrol. We can see that it could also be done with modest footwear.

26

Ein Sonnenbad am Großglockner Anfang der 1960er. Die imposante Berglandschaft ist immer eine Pause wert.

Rechte Seite: Ein Bergsteiger in Zivilkleidung, stilgerecht mit umgebundener Fliege. Der faszinierende Blick vom Großglockner nahe der Kaiser-Franz-Josephs-Höhe um 1961.

Sunbathing on the Großglockner at the beginning of the nineteen-sixties. It is always worth taking a break for this impressive mountain landscape.

Right page: a mountaineer in civilian clothing, appropriately dressed with a self-tied bow tie. The fascinating view from the Großglockner close to the Kaiser-Franz-Josephs-Höhe around 1961.

28

Idylle in Johnsbach 1961.

Rechte Seite: Ein kerniger Bergbauer auf einer Tiroler Alm. Irgendwann in den 1960ern.

Idyll in Johnsbach in 1961.

Right page: an earthy miner on a Tyrol Alpine pasture. Some time in the 1960s.

30

Zeitreise ins Jahr 1962. Die Gondelbahn von der Roßhütte bei Seefeld aufs Seefelder Joch unter der Seefelder Spitze.

A journey through time to 1962. The cable car from the Roßhütte near Seefeld to the Seefelder Joch beneath the Seefelder Spitze.

2

32

Mit dem nagelneuen Fiat 600 in den 1950ern die Alpen erkunden.

Rechte Seite: Für den sonntäglichen Kirchgang ist im Tirol der 1960er traditionelle Tracht mit Haarreifen aus Spitzen Pflicht.

Exploring the Alps in the brand new Fiat 600 in the nineteen-fifties.

Right page: in the Tyrol of the 1960s tradtional costume with lace hair bands is compulsory for going to church on Sundays.

Linke Seite: An dieser Stelle befindet sich heute der Speichersee Durlaßboden am Gerlospass, dahinter sieht man die Wildkarspitze (3073m).

Unten: Dieses Foto aus dem Jahr 1947 ist mit „Mit dem Taxi zum Großglockner" beschriftet. Dem ist nicht viel hinzuzufügen, außer ein wunderbarer Blick hinab ins Käfertal.

Left page: today the Durlaßboden reservoir on the Gerlos Pass stands at this point; behind it the Wildkarspitze can be seen (3073 m).

Below: this photograph from 1947 bears the inscription: "By taxi to the Großglockner". There is little to be added to this, apart from a wonderful view down into the Käfertal.

36

Die typischen Erinnerungen an idyllische Landurlaube aus Kindertagen Mitte der 1960er. Aus heutiger Sicht eine pastellfarbene Zeitreise, für Knirpse damals oft eine Qual: stundenlange Wanderungen mit den Eltern.

The typical memories of childhood days on idyllic country holidays in the mid-sixties. A pastel-coloured journey through time from today's perspective, for little fellows at the time it was often torture: going walking for hours with your parents.

38

Nicht viel los in Rattenberg, 1965.

Not much going on in Rattenberg, 1965.

Unten: Den schnittigen Silberpfeil am Wegrand geparkt, konnte man 1968 – und natürlich auch heute noch – in Ruhe die erfrischende Luft auf der Alm in Tirol genießen. Offensichtlich galt das Interesse des Fotografen hier eher dem Automobil als der Natur.

Rechte Seite: Knickerbocker, dicke Strümpfe, hohe Schnürstiefel gehörten zur Grundausstattung für jede Wanderung. Hier posiert der junge Mann im Jahr 1961 in den Zillertaler Alpen für das obligate Erinnerungsfoto.

Below: with your stylish silver arrow parked at the wayside you could enjoy the refreshing air in the Alpine pasture in Tyrol in 1968 – as you still can today, of course. Here the photographer's interest obviously lay more in the motor car than in the scenery.

Right page: plus-fours, thick socks and high lace-up boots were part of the basic equipment for every walk. Here the young man poses in the Zillertal Alps for the obligatory keepsake photograph in 1961.

Wackeliges Fischervergnügen in den 1970er-Jahren.

Rechte Seite: Tiroler Almidylle samt Gebirgsfahrzeug. Zu sehen die Ladiz-Alm mit Blick auf die Herzogkante im Jahr 1969.

Shaky fishing fun in the seventies.

Right page: Tyrolean Alpine pasture idyll along with mountain vehicle. The Ladiz-Alm Alpine pasture is seen here with a view of the Herzogkante in 1969.

ERH-S 777

44

Einmal mehr die liebgewonnene norwegische Familie 1963 auf ausgedehnter Sommerurlaubsrundreise quer durch Österreich. Die wohlverdiente Rast in der Nassfelder Gegend.

Rechte Seite: Der Größe nach aufgestellt, dient die sympathische Familie als beliebtes Fotomotiv vor der malerischen Naturkulisse.

Once again the Norwegian family of whom we have become so fond, here in 1963 on an extended summer holiday tour through Austria. Well-earned rest in the Nassfeld area.

Right page: stood in height order, the likeable family serves as a photographic subject in front of the picturesque natural scenery.

Unten: Wieder eine Zwischenetappe absolviert. Papa lichtet noch rasch seine Lieblinge ab, bevor die Reise irgendwann Anfang 1960 weitergeht.

Rechte Seite oben: Herrliche Aussicht von der Hohen Wand anno 1963.

Rechte Seite unten: Der Blick der neugierigen Wanderer auf die von Nebel verhüllte Bischofsmütze in Salzburg im Sommer 1959.

Below: one more stage completed. Dad just squeezes in one more photo of his darlings before the journey (some time at the beginning of the 1960s) continues.

Right page, above: magnificent view of the Hohe Wand in 1963.

Right page, below: the curious walkers' view of the Bischofsmütze in Salzburg cloaked in fog in summer 1959.

Kl. Kanzel

48

Skeptische Blicke unterm Marterl. Sommerurlaub in den 1960er-Jahren.

Rechte Seite: Auch in den Bergen kann die Sommerhitze unerträglich werden wie offenbar auch im Jahr 1958. Was liegt da näher, als gleich in den nächsten Dorfbrunnen zu springen wie diese drei Burschen in Going, Tirol?

Sceptical looks beneath the wayside shrine. Summer holiday in the nineteen-sixties.

Right page: the summer heat can also become unbearable in the mountains, just as it obviously was in 1958. What could then be more obvious than to jump straight into the nearest village well like these three fellows in Going, Tyrol?

50

„Der Großglockner ist mehr als der höchste Berg Österreichs – ihn umstrahlt das Fluidum einer ungewöhnlichen Persönlichkeit. Wer in seinen Bannkreis gerät, wird davon erfasst.“ Oskar Kühlken
Höhe: 3.798 Meter | Erstbesteigung: 1800
Alpenstraße: 48 Kilometer, 36 Kehren

Unten: Freie Fahrt für freie Bürger, ca. 1965.

"The Großglockner is more than the highest mountain in Austria – an aura of unusual personality radiates around it. Whoever enters its influence is grabbed by it."
Oskar Kühlken
Height: 3,798 metres | first ascent: 1800
Alpine road: 48 kilometres, 36 bends

Below: Green light for free citizens, approx. 1965

Eröffnung der Großglockner Hochalpenstraße, 1935.

Opening of the Großglockner high altitude Alpine road, 1935.

Was für eine Naturkulisse für ein Erinnerungsfoto anno 1965. Der obligate Käfer auf der Großglocknerstraße, strahlender Sonnenschein und eine glückliche Familie.

What natural scenery for a memento photograph in 1965. The obligatory beetle on the Großglocknerstraße, radiant sunshine and a happy family.

Die Europabrücke, ein Wunderwerk der Technik. Sie bildet das Kernstück der österreichischen Brenner-Autobahn und überspannt in 190 Meter Höhe das Wipptal zwischen Patsch und Schönberg. Seit 1963 fließt hier der Verkehr Richtung Südtirol, vorher war der Weg in die Dolomiten eine kleine Weltreise.

The Europabrücke, an engineering marvel. It forms the core piece of the Austrian Brenner Motorway and spans the Wipp Valley between Patsch and Schönberg at a height of 190 metres. Traffic headed for South Tyrol has been travelling across it since 1963; before this the route to the Dolomites took you halfway around the world.

Unten: Sommer, Sonne und ein herzhaftes Lächeln für die Kamera. Später geborene Generationen würden den Stil der 1960er übrigens heute wohl als „Mad Men"-Style bezeichnen. Neben dem formschönen Automobil beachte man das Brillendesign!

Rechte Seite: Zeitreise ins Jahr 1963. Eine kurze Rast wird vom Herrn Papa gleich für einen Schnappschuss genützt. Im Hintergrund das Tennengebirge, am Bildrand links ein Ford Taunus.

Below: summer, sunshine and a broad smile for the camera. Those belonging to later-born generations today just might describe the look of the sixties as "Mad Men" style. Along with the elegant motor car one also notes the design of the spectacles!

Right page: a journey through time to 1963. Father makes use of a short rest to take a snap too. In the background are the Tennen Mountains; at the edge of the picture on the left is a Ford Taunus.

P

Unten: Die Krefelder Hütte, Salzburg 1963.

Rechte Seite: Traumhaftes Alpenpanorama anno 1960.

Below: the Krefelder Hütte / Salzburg in 1963.

Right page: fantastic Alpine panorama in 1960.

58

Lief der Motor zu heiß, hieß es Kühlerhaube auf und lüften. Das war die Gelegenheit für ein gemütliches Picknick am Wegesrand. Man hatte ja zum Glück alles dabei, von der Thermoskanne bis zur Keksdose. Um 1930.

If the engine was running too hot that meant opening the bonnet to air it. This was the chance for a leisurely wayside picnic. Of course luckily one had everything on hand, from the thermos flask right through to the biscuit tin. Approx. 1930.

Unten: Ja, solch steinigen Monumenten und Denkmälern begegnet man als fleißiger Wanderer in luftiger Höhe.

Rechte Seite: Doch auch der fleißigste Wanderer braucht einmal eine Pause, Mitte der 1970er-Jahre.

Yes, on strenuous walks at a dizzy height you will come across stony monuments and memorials like these.

Right page: but even those used to the most strenuous walks need the occasional break (mid-nineteen-seventies).

62

Will man von der rauen Schweiz ins mediterrane Italien, nimmt man den Gotthardpass. Vier Möglichkeiten gibt es hier: die Eisenbahn, den Autobahntunnel, die Bundesstraße und die alte Poststraße durch das Val Tremola. Im Albergo San Gottardo und im Hospiz nächtigten schon einige Promis wie Charles Dickens und Victor Hugo.

If you want to go from bleak Switzerland into Mediterranean Italy you take the Gotthard Pass. There are four options here: the railway, the motorway tunnel, the highway or the old post road through Val Tremola. The Albergo San Gottardo and the Hospiz have previously accommodated several celebs like Charles Dickens and Victor Hugo.

Der St. Gotthardpass in der Schweiz, in den 1950er-Jahren.

The St. Gotthard Pass in Switzerland, in the nineteen-fifties.

Unten: Hilfesuchende Blicke Mitte 1970: Auf welchem Gipfel befinde ich mich?

Rechts: Alpenerkundungstour mit einem Opel Rekord P1 irgendwann in den 1960ern. Zu sehen die Langkofelgruppe am Sellajoch in Südtirol.

Below: looking for assistance in the mid-seventies: which peak am I on?

Right: Alpine reconnaissance trip with an Opel Rekord P1 some time in the nineteen-sixties. We can see the Langkofel Group on the Sella Pass in South Tyrol.

A
W7·229

Nach dem Aufstieg das Foto in Siegerpose, dann endlich Ruhe und Entspannung für ihn, während sie den Triumph noch auskosten muss (siehe Seite 68).

After the climb comes the photograph in a victory pose, then peace and relaxation are finally his, whilst she still needs to make the most of the triumph (see page 68).

68

Nach dem Foto in Siegerpose träumt sie von einem Bad in einem kalten Bergsee. Um 1975.

After the photograph in a victory pose comes the dream of taking a swimm in a cold mountain lake. Approx. 1975

70

Wer meint, die Flitterwochen kann man nur im Süden verbringen, lässt sich vielleicht von dieser Aufnahme vom Gegenteil überzeugen. Auf Hochzeitsreise in den Lienzer Dolomiten im Jahr 1962 posiert die frisch gebackene Ehefrau vor der Flitterwochenhütte. Da kommt Romantik auf.

Those who think honeymoons can only be spent in southern climes might be persuaded to the contrary by this shot. The newly-wed poses in front of the marital lodge whilst on her honeymoon in the Lienz Dolomites. It evokes romance.

Sehnsucht nach einem Besuch des Millstätter Sees kommt beim Anblick dieser wunderbaren Aufnahme aus dem Jahr 1961 auf. Schwer zu entscheiden, was uns besser gefällt: Die idyllische Berglandschaft im Hintergrund, das Wasser, auf dem die Boote im Wind schaukeln oder die zwei jungen Damen, die da an der Brüstung sitzen und in die Kamera lächeln?

A longing for a visit to Lake Millstatt is what is evoked by a look at this wonderful shot from 1961. Hard to decide what we like the most: the idyllic mountain landscape in the background, the water with the boats rocking in the wind, or the two young ladies sitting there on the railings and smiling at the camera?

Unten: Erste Schwimmversuche mit Papa im Sommerurlaub am Schwarzensee im Salzkammergut. Mitte der 1960er-Jahre waren die Schwimmflügel zwar schon erfunden, aber die Luftmatratze tut's auch.

Rechte Seite: Aufnahme einer idyllischen Berghütte in Schwaz in Tirol in den 1960er-Jahren.

Below: first attempts at swimming with Dad on a summer holiday at the Schwarzensee in the Salzkammergut. Although water wings had already been invented by the mid-sixties, the air mattress can also do the job.

Right page: shot of an idyllic mountain lodge in Schwaz in Tyrol in the sixties.

Unten: Sommerurlaub mit der ganzen Familie in Schwaz in Tirol Ende der 1960er-Jahre. Die Kinder tragen natürlich selbstgenähte Dirndlkleider.

Rechte Seite: Aussichtsplattform auf der Schafbergspitze, in den frühen 1960er-Jahren.

Below: summer holiday with the whole family in Schwaz in Tyrol at the end of the nineteen-sixties. The children are wearing dirndls they made themselves, of course.

Right page: viewing platform on the Schafbergspitze, in the early nineteen-sixties.

76

Unten: Posieren wie die Großen beim Sonntagsausflug im nagelneuen Ford Taunus. Die perfekte Gelegenheit, um endlich einmal den Beifahrersitz zu okkupieren und sich den Bergwind durch das Haar wehen zu lassen!

Posing like the grown-ups on a Sunday outing in a brand new Ford Taunus. The perfect chance finally to occupy the front passenger seat for once, and let the mountain wind blow through your hair!

Oben: An einem der zahlreichen schönen Alpenseen Mitte der 1960er-Jahre.

Unten: Familienurlaub am Bauernhof in Schwaz in Tirol im Jahr 1968.

Above; at one of the many beautiful Alpine lakes in the mid-nineteen-sixties.

Below: family holiday on a farm in Schwaz in Tyrol in 1968.

Unten: Praktisch ungesichert durchs Gebirgsgeröll um 1975.

Rechte Seite: Sommerfrische Anfang der 1960er in Flirsch am Arlberg. Für ein paar Tage der Stadt entfliehen und frische Landluft genießen.

Below: through the mountain scree with virtually no safety equipment around 1975.

Right page: summer getaway at the beginning of the sixties in Flirsch on the Arlberg. Escaping from the town and enjoying fresh country air for a few days.

A
W7-229

80

Dichte Nebeldecken über den Tälern sind stets begehrte Fotomotive für jeden Bergsteiger. Das Geschenk nach dem anstrengenden Aufstieg: ein atemberaubender Ausblick.

Thick blankets of fog over the valleys are always a much sought-after photographic subject for all mountaineers. The gift after the strenuous climb: a breathtaking view.

Das sagenumwobene Gebiet der Fanes hat ein besonderes Flair. Der Falzaregopass ist ein breiter, mit Felsbrocken übersäter Sattel in der Provinz Belluno und verbindet Buchenstein (ladinisch: Fodom) mit Cortina d'Ampezzo. Hier soll der falsche König (falza rego) der Sage nach wegen seines Verrates zu Stein erstarrt sein. Man sieht ihn noch heute vom Pass aus am Lagazuoi. Um 1970.

The legendary Fanes region has a special atmosphere. The Falzarego Pass is a wide saddle strewn with rocks in the Province of Belluno, and connects Buchenstein (Ladin: Fodom) with Cortina d'Ampezzo. According to the legend the false king (falza rego) froze into stone for his treason. He can still be seen today from the pass at Lagazuoi. Approx. 1970.

ALBERGO FALZAREGO

84

Am höchsten Punkt des Falzaregopasses (Italien) steht diese kleine Kapelle. Dahinter der Hexenstein. Hier verlief im Ersten Weltkrieg die Gebirgsfront, wo es ab 1916 zu einem unerbittlichen Minenkampf zwischen Österreichern und Italienern kam. Auf diesem Fotos aber rund 60 Jahre später.

This little chapel stands at the highest point of the Falzarego Pass (Italy). Behind it is the Hexenstein. In the First World War the mountain front passed through here, and 1916 saw the start of merciless mine warfare between Austrians and Italians. But these photographs show it around sixty years later.

Unten: Einige der tapferen Maurer rund um Celeste Dellantonio, die in den 1920-Jahren in lebensgefährlicher Knochenarbeit Hotels für Touristen gebaut hatten. Hier auf einem Foto Ende der 1920er am San Pellegrino Pass.

Rechts unten: Sommer 1959, Ausflug auf die Aualm, im Hintergrund die Bischofsmütze. Für Autofans: ja, das ist eine BMW Isetta.

Below: a few of the brave bricklayers around Celeste Dellantonio, who risked their lives building hotels for tourists in the twenties. Here in a photograph at the end of the nineteen-twenties at the San Pellegrino Pass.

Below right: summer 1959, trip to the Aualm with the Bischofsmütze in the background. For car fans: yes, that is a BMW Isetta.

Sommer 1965, Kolbnitz im Mölltal mit Danielsberg, dahinter die Hohen Tauern.

Summer 1965, Kolbnitz in the Mölltal valley, together with the Danielsberg, and the Hohe Tauern behind them.

Unten: Alpenidylle anno 1970. Die Bildbeschriftung erzählt uns „Wanderung mit Onkel Fritz“, samt Belichtungs-Insekt.

Rechte Seite: Die Pfarrkirche in Elbigenalb im Lechtal, abgelichtet im Jahr 1971.

Below: Alpine idyll in 1970. The picture's inscription says, "A walk with Uncle Fritz", complete with exposed insect.

Right page: the parish church in Elbigenalb in the Lechtal taken in 1971.

Der Blick auf die Wetterspitze im Tiroler Lechtal im Jahr 1971.

The view down to the Wetterspitze in the Lechtal in Tyrol in 1971.

92

Aus der Prä-Google-Earth-Ära. Drei Landvermesser (ein Kartograph mit seinen beiden Gehilfen) bei der Arbeit im Lechtal 1971. Losgezogen mit lediglich einem weißen Blatt Papier haben sie unglaubliche Leistungen vollbracht. Am Foto zu sehen ist übrigens auch das Mädelejoch.

From the pre-Google Earth era. Three land surveyors (a cartographer with both of his assistants) at work in the Lechtal in 1971. Having set out with only a sheet of paper their achievements have been incredible. Incidentally, the Mädelejoch is also visible in the photograph.

Oben: Mit dem Motorrad 1964 unterwegs zum wilden Kaiser, der im Bildhintergrund majestätisch emporragt.

Unten: Wochenendausflug auf der Rax Richtung Ottohaus im Jahr 1959.

Above: travelling by motorcycle in 1964 to the Wilder Kaiser, rising up majestically in the background of the picture.

Below: a weekend trip on the Rax towards Ottohaus in 1959.

Unten: Eine Aufnahme wie aus dem Bilderbuch. Alpen-Edelweiß, begehrtes Fotoobjekt jedes Wanderers.

Rechte Seite: Rückblick ins Jahr 1962. Zu sehen der Tegernsee mit dem Ort Rottach-Egern und der St. Laurentius-Kirche.

Below: a shot as if from a picture book. Alpine edelweiß, just as every walker likes to photograph it.

Right page: a look back to 1962. Here we see the Tegernsee with the municipality of Rottach-Egern and the Church of St. Laurentius.

G939

Unten: Am Weg in die Sommerfrische in den 1960ern.

Rechte Seite: Das Hotel Valentin neben der Gaislachkogelbahn in Sölden 1962. Mittlerweile wurden Hotel und Bahn massiv ausgebaut.

Below: on the way to a summer getaway in the nineteen-sixties.

Right page: the Hotel Valentin next to the Gaislachkogel cable car in Sölden in 1962. Since then the Hotel and the cable car have been considerably extended.

HOTEL PENS
VALENTIN

Rechte Seite: Lienzer Dolomiten 1962

Right page: Lienz Dolomites 1962

Besuch eines typischen Bauernhauses, nach einer anstrengenden Wanderung. 1964.

Visiting a typical Austrian Farmhouse after an exhausting hike. 1964.

Unten: Lienzer Dolomiten 1962: Die richtige Bekleidung beim Wandern gehörte dazu wie das Amen im Gebet. Nur mit Knickerbockern, selbstgestrickten Kniestrümpfen und dem obligatorischen Lodenwalker war der Berg bezwingbar. Und im Partnerlook machte es gleich doppelt so viel Spaß.

Rechte Seite: Beim Spaziergang mit den Großeltern in Mitterbach am Erlaufsee im Jahr 1968.

Below: the Lienz Dolomites in 1962: the right clothing was as much a part of walking as the "amen" in a prayer. The mountain could only be overcome with plus-fours, home-knitted knee-length socks and the obligatory Lodenwalker. And in his and hers versions it was instantly twice as much fun.

Right page: on a stroll with grandparents in Mitterbach on the Erlaufsee in 1968.

Linke Seite: Bummel durch die Innsbrucker Innenstadt, Juli 1930.

Unten: Philosophieren am Gipfel in den 1960er-Jahren.

Left page: stroll through the Innsbruck town centre, July 1930.

Below: philosphising at the summit in the nineteen-sixties.

Oben: Ein Wanderer genießt die Ruhe und Rauchpause in Ramsau am Dachstein 1959.

Unten: Lächeln fürs Familienfotoalbum in Seefeld in Tirol 1956.

Above: a walker enjoying the peace and a tobacco break in Ramsau am Dachstein in 1959.

Below: smiling for the family photograph album in Seefeld in Tyrol in 1956.

Auf der steirischen Tauplitz-Alm in den 1970ern.

In the Tauplitz Alpine pasture, Styria, in the seventies.

Links: Ein Foto aus dem Jahr 1962. Zu sehen ist der Inn bei Schwaz in Tirol.

Rechts: Ob 1961 oder heute: Eine Fahrt über den schönen Millstätter See sollte man sich trotz der spärlich vorhandenen Rettungsringe, die wohl eher zu dekorativen Zwecken am Schiff angebracht sind, nicht entgehen lassen.

Left: a photograph from 1962. The view is of the River Inn at Schwaz in Tyrol.

Right: whether in 1961 or today: a trip across the beautiful Lake Millstatt is not to be missed, despite the sparse availability of the life rings, probably mounted on the ship for decorative purposes.

108

Während die Cousine dem Vater brav bei der Gartenarbeit half (rechte Seite), ruhten wir Burschen uns vom Nichtstun aus. Mitte der 1970er-Jahre.

Whilst our cousin helpfully assisted father with the gardening (right page) we fellows took a rest after being busy doing nothing. Mid-nineteen-seventies.

110

St. Christoph am Arlberg in den 1970er-Jahren. Ferienlager mit Kaplan Hans Bensdorp, als es noch die gleichnamigen Schokoladeriegel gab.

St. Christoph am Arlberg in the nineteen-seventies. A holiday camp with chaplain Hans Bensdorp, at the time when his chocolate bar namesake was still available.

Unten: Früh übt sich, wer ein Jägersmann sein möchte. Mitte der 1970er-Jahre.

Rechte Seite: Gastgartenromantik vor der Kulisse des Wilden Kaisers, 1965.

Below: early practice makes perfect if you want to be a huntsman! From the mid-nineteen-seventies.

Right page: romantic beer garden with the Wilder Kaiser as a backdrop, 1965.

KEGELBAHN

Nach einem herzhaften Mittagessen am Tag des Herren ging es weiter in die Berge mit dem schnittigen VW-Käfer. Dem Schuhwerk nach zu schließen aber ohne sportliche Komponente. 1976.

Following a hearty lunch on the Lord's Day it was on into the mountains in the stylish VW beetle. But judging by the footwear nothing sporty was planned. 1976.

Entspannte Kindheit am Ritten in Südtirol. Das Dirndl gehört zum Sommerfrischen-Look. Von hier aus gibt's den besten Blick auf den Schlern. 1968.

Auch Queen Elizabeth II. besuchte 1969 die Alpen. Hier mit Landeshauptmann Eduard Wallnöfer flankiert von einer Schützenkompanie.

Relaxed childhood on the Ritten in South Tyrol. The dirndl is part of the summer getaway look. The best view of the Schlern is from here. Approx. 1966.

In 1969 even Queen Elizabeth II visited the Alps. Seen here with Landeshauptmann Eduard Wallnöfer flanked by a Schützenkompanie.

118

Die ganze Kinderschar in den Kübelwagen gepackt und los geht's von Oberbozen nach Klobenstein am Ritten. Im Hintergrund das wuchtige Schlernmassiv. Ende der 1960er-Jahre

The whole gaggle of children is packed into the jeep and off we go from Oberbozen to Klobenstein am Ritten. In the background is the heavy Schlern massif. This is at the end of the nineteen-sixties.

In den 1960er-Jahren war die Welt des klassischen Opel-Fahrers noch in Ordnung.

In the nineteen-sixties all was still well in the world of the classic Opel driver.

Oben: Auf den steilen Wiesen heißt es, den Ball festhalten. Wen interessiert da das Reich von König Laurin, der schneebedeckte Rosengarten?

Unten: Ballspielen vor den Dolomiten, Ende der 1960er-Jahre.

Above: when you are on the steep grassy areas you need to keep hold of the ball. Who is going to be interested in King Laurin's empire, the snow-covered rose garden, up there?

Below: ball games in front of the Dolomites at the end of the nineteen-sixties.

Bequem im Autoreisezug bis an den Urlaubsort in den 1960ern. Vor allem während der Ölkrise 1973 eine begehrte Transportform.

In comfort all the way to the holiday resort on a motorail train in the sixties. This form of transport was especially sought-after during the oil crisis in 1973.

Auf einer Strecke von 110 Kilometern verbindet die Gotthardstraße den Kanton Uri mit dem Tessin. Auf der Passhöhe überquert sie die Wasserscheide zwischen Rhein und Po, um 1976.

A 110-kilometre stretch of the Gotthardstraße connects the Cantons of Uri and Ticino. Here it is crossing the watershed between the Rhine and the Po at pass altitude, approx. 1976.

126

Mitte der 1970er-Jahre am Rigi. Die traditionell gehisste Schweizer Flagge war es nicht, was die Schwester zum skeptischen Blick veranlasste.

Mid-nineteen-seventies on Rigi. It was not the traditionally hoisted Swiss flag that brought about the sceptical look from sister.

Zeitreise ins Jahr 1955. Auf dem Weg durch das Rhonetal aufwärts von Martigny nach Sion in der Schweiz. Eine kurze Rast mit Stärkung und zur Orientierung inmitten der sogenannten „Kornmandln".

A journey through time to 1955. On the way through the Rhone Valley, ascending from Martigny to Sion in Switzerland. A short rest for refreshments and to get bearings in the midst of the so-called "Kornmandln".

AUS DEN ALBEN DER ERINNERUNG

FROM THE ALBUMS OF MEMORY

Ausschnitte aus einem Fotoalbum aus Zell am See, Kaprun und Umgebung.
Excerpts from a photograph album from Zell am See, Kaprun and the surrounding area.

Linke Seite oben: Original beschriftet mit „Kesselfall Alpenhaus, 1056 m, 22. Juni 1904“.

Linke Seite unten: Originalbeschriftung „Achental mit Glocknerkaar Gruppe“ anno 1904.

Unten: Einsamer Bergsteiger im Hang anno 1904.

Left page, above: originally inscribed with "Kessellfall Alpenhaus, 1056 m, 22nd June 1904".

Left page, below: original inscription "Achental with Glocknerkaar Group", 1904.

Below: lone mountaineer on slope, 1904.

Ausschnitte aus dem Fotoalbum Alpenüberquerung anno 1924

Excerpts from Photograph Album Alpine crossing, 1924

Ausschnitt aus einem faszinierenden, privaten Fotoalbum. Im Jahr 1924 brach eine Reisegesellschaft zwischen 10. Juli und 17. August 1924 auf, um die Alpen von Österreich aus zu überqueren und nach Italien zu gelangen. Ein besonderes Abenteuer, da es mit dem Automobil über schmale Schotterwege und Straßen ging.

Unten: Die Reisegesellschaft genießt den atemberaubenden Ausblick vom Franz-Josefs-Haus am Großglockner.

Excerpt from a fascinating personal photograph album. In 1924 a party set out to reach Italy by crossing the Alps from the Austrian side between the 10th of July and the 17th of August. This was particularly adventurous, since the motor car would be travelling over narrow gravel tracks and roads.

Below: the party enjoying the breathtaking view from Franz-Joseph's-house on the Großglockner.

Nach erfolgreicher Alpenüberquerung genießt die Reisegesellschaft das italienische Strandleben und die Sonne.

After a successful Alpine crossing the party enjoy the sun and life on an Italian beach.

DIE ENTDECKUNG DES WINTER-SPORTS

THE DISCOVERY OF WINTER SPORT

AUTRICHE

Ab den 1950er- Jahren entwickelte sich das Schifahren zum Massensport. Seilbahnen und Schilifte wurden gebaut, Pisten planiert und Schihütten eröffnet. Der Wintertourismus in den Alpen boomte. Schlepplifte gab es allerdings schon früher, den Pionier 1934 in Davos. Der erste Bügellift hieß übrigens „Sie-und-Er-Lift".
Mit dem Schlepplift auf die Seiseralm in den 1960ern. Skispaß und ein traumhafter Ausblick waren auch damals schon die Belohnung.

From the nineteen-fifties onwards skiing developed into a popular mass sport. Cable cars and ski lifts were built, pistes were levelled off and ski lodges were opened. In the Alps, winter tourism boomed. In fact there had already been ski tows earlier, pioneered in Davos in 1934. The first T-bar ski lift, incidentally, was called the "His and Hers Lift".
By tow lift on the Seiseralm in the sixties. Skiing fun and a fantastic view were the reward, even back then.

Der Langkofel und Plattkofel in den Dolomiten. Eine wundervolle Naturkulisse und Alpenidylle anno 1960.
Auch Langlaufen und Schitourengehen erfreute sich wachsender Beliebtheit. Loipen wurden lange Zeit von Langläufern angelegt, die als erste ihre Spuren durch den unberührten Schnee zogen.

Unten: Ein fotografisches Juwel aus den 1960ern. Die mühsamen letzten Schritte zum Gipfelkreuz auf der Wildspitze (3.768m), dem zweithöchsten Berg Österreichs.

The Langkofel and Plattkofel in the Dolomites. Wonderful natural scenery and an Alpine idyll in 1960. Cross-country skiing and ski touring were also enjoying increasing popularity. For a long time it was cross-country skiers, first to leave tracks through the untouched snow, who laid out trails.

Below: a photographic jewel from the sixties. The arduous final steps to the cross on the summit of the Wildspitze (3,768 m), the second highest mountain in Austria.

Aufstieg geschafft! Die Fotos entstanden im Juli 1930 in Tirol amHafelekar

Ascent completed! The photographs were created in July 1930 on the Hafelekar in Tyrol.

144

„Onkel Heinzi Skiurlaub Mitte 1960“ lautet die originale Bildbeschriftung. Das Foto zeigt Obertauern und den Parkplatz der Zehnerkar Seilbahn.

Rechte Seite: Ein Schnappschuss anno 1949. Nach dem anstrengenden Aufstieg genießt die junge Dame offensichtlich die wohlverdiente Sonne am Dachstein.

"Uncle Heinzi skiing holiday mid-seventies" reads the picture's original inscription. The photograph shows Obertauern and the Zehnerkar cable car car park.

Right page: a snap from 1949. Following the strenuous ascent the young lady is obviously enjoying the well-earned sunshine on the Dachstein.

Unten: Tiroler Stilleben mit Kuh, Hafelekar 1930.

Rechte Seite: Familienfoto auf der nagelneuen Rodel in St. Johann in Tirol Ende der 60er-Jahre.

Below: Tyrolean still life with cow, Hafelekar 1930.

Right page: family photograph on the brand new toboggan in St. Johann in Tyrol at the end of the sixties.

Keilhosen waren bis Ende der 1960er-Jahre en vogue. Ihr Erfinder war ein bescheidener Schneider aus Tirol, der für sich sebst eine möglichst windschlüpfrige Hose nähte.

Ski pants were in vogue until the end of the nineteen-sixties. Their inventor was a modest tailor from Tyrol, who made himself a pair of trousers to be as streamlined as possible.

Schneemann bauen bei Bad Hofgastein im Staatsvertragsjahr 1955.

Building a snowman near Bad Hofgastein in the year of the Austrian State Treaty.

Auf Skiurlaub in St. Johann in Tirol im Jahr 1968. Die ersten Stehversuche auf Skiern, gar nicht so einfach, wie das bei der Mama aussieht.

On a skiing holiday in St. Johann in Tyrol in 1968. First attempts at standing upright on skis, nothing like as simple as it looks for Mum.

150

Im Norwegerpulli und Pudelmütze ging's in den Schnee hinaus. Der dicke Pullover mit dem typischen Muster stammte eigentlich aus Island und gelangte in den 1970er-Jahren nach Österreich.

Off out into the snow in a Norwegian jumper and bobble hat. In fact the thick pullover with the typical pattern originated in Iceland, and arrived in Austria in the nineteen-seventies.

Schifahren mit Knickerbocker, Stutzen und für heutige Verhältnisse außergewöhnlichen Kopfbedeckungen in St. Moritz anno 1926.

Skiing in plus-fours, stirrup socks and headgear which is unusual by today's standards in St. Moritz in 1926.

Unten: Ostern 1932. Winterspaß und frühe Skisprungversucne am Draugstein in Salzburg.

Rechte Seite: Ostern 1936. Schnappschuss von der Wanderung auf die steirische Tauplitzalm.

Below: Easter 1932. Winter fun and early attempts at ski jumping on the Draugstein in Salzburg.

Right page: Easter 1936. Snap from a walk to the Tauplitzalm in Styria.

Unten: Die Kitzbüheler Hornbahn um 1951.

Rechte Seite: Lächeln für die Kamera vor der Gondelfahrt auf den Berg, in den frühen 1930ern.

Below: the Kitzbühel Horn cable car around 1951.

Right page: smiling for the camera before the cable car trip up the mountain in the early thirties.

Englische Übersetzung: Anthony Creaton
Logo-Gestaltung „Vintage Alps“: Rudolf Ehrenreich

Bildnachweis:
Idar Johannessen/Hans Einar Johannessen Privatarchiv: S. 9, 12-19, 30-31, 36-37, 44-46, 54-55, 94-97, 138-141; Josef Föger/Berthold Föger Privatarchiv: S. 20 oben, S 28 rechts, S 32 rechts; Familie Mauracher Privatarchiv: S. 20 unten, S 40-41, S 43; Conrad Seidl: S. 24-27; Privatarchiv Schipany: S. 28, 56, 79, 87 rechts unten, S. 113; Florian Schwarz Privatarchiv: S. 32, 34; Franz Seyringer Privatarchiv: S. 35, 126 rechts; Walter Ludwig Privatarchiv: S 46, 49, 103 rechts oben, rechts unten, 148 unten; Michael Klemsch Privatarchiv: S 51 unten; E. Müller-Schreiber Privatarchiv: S 56, 58-59, 60-61, 62-63, 64, 65, 78, 79, 80-81, 82-83, 84, 85, 103 links; Privatarchiv Dellantonio: S. 86; Paul Golger Privatarchiv: S. 87 oben; Rudolf Ehrenreich Privatarchiv: S. 88, 144; T. Müllner Privatarchiv: S. 89, 90-91, 92, 93; Privatarchiv Christoph Lütge: S. 102, 142, 143, 146; Ursula Ressl Privatarchiv: S. 123; Sammlung Wolfgang Weihs: S. 130 – 135; Sabine Egger Privatarchiv: S. 145; Familie Singer Privatarchiv: S. 152, 153; Christian Rösner-El Heliebi Privatarchiv: S. 154, 155; Wolfgang Bauer Privatarchiv: S. 156; Hedwig Schaner Privatarchiv: S. 157; Archiv Metroverlag: S. 10-11, S. 21-22, 39, 42, 48, 50, 51 oben, S. 52-53, 66-69, 70-77, 98-99, 100-101, 104-105, 106-107, 108-109, 110-112, 114-115, 116, 117, 118, 119, 120-121, 122 oben/unten, 124-125, 126, 147, 149, 150, 151

Ein herzliches Dankeschön an alle, die uns für dieses Buch- & Blogprojekt mit Fotos aus dem eigenen Privat- & Familienarchiv unterstützt haben. Besonderer Dank gilt auch jenen, die Vintage Alps mit ihrem wertvollen Beitrag ein Stück des Weges begleitet und von Beginn an mitgeformt haben (in alphabetischer Reihenfolge):
Hans Einar Johannessen, Rudolf Ehrenreich, Wolfgang Weihs und das gesamte Metroverlag-Team.

www.vintagealps.at

Verlagsbüro W. GmbH.
info@metroverlag.at

Printed in the EU
ISBN 978-3-99300-170-4